Masked/
Unmuted

poems by

Jean Hackett

Finishing Line Press
Georgetown, Kentucky

Masked/
Unmuted

Copyright © 2022 by Jean Hackett
ISBN 978-1-64662-786-8 First Edition
All rights reserved under International and Pan-American Copyright Conventions. No part of this book may be reproduced in any manner whatsoever without written permission from the publisher, except in the case of brief quotations embodied in critical articles and reviews.

ACKNOWLEDGMENTS

Beached, published as Sirens, *Langdon Review*, 2020
Living in the Moment, *Tejascovido*, 2020
March 15, 2020, *Voices de la Luna*, 2020
Mice, *No Season for Silence*, 2020
Peace and Harmony, *Tejascovido*, 2020
Rant, *No Season for Silence*, 2020
Sax Man, *No Season for Silence*, 2020
Supermarket Vision of Hell, *No Season for Silence*, 2020
The Not So Maddening Crowd, *ArtsAlive SA*, 2020
View from my Window, *No Season for Silence*, 2020

Publisher: Leah Huete de Maines
Editor: Christen Kincaid
Cover Art: Jean Hackett
Author Photo: Robert Wilkes
Cover Design: Elizabeth Maines McCleavy

Order online: www.finishinglinepress.com
       also available on amazon.com

Author inquiries and mail orders:
Finishing Line Press
PO Box 1626
Georgetown, Kentucky 40324
USA

Table of Contents

Peace and Harmony 1
March 15, 2020 2
Out West 3
The Plague 4
Feminine Protection 5
Angst and Apprehension 6
Supermarket vision of Hell..7
Mice..8
Living in the Moment 9
José Posada, Sax Man at Central Market...10
View from my Window 11
The Not So Maddening Crowd 12
Another Kind of Tragedy 13
Rant 14
Out of Santa Fe 15
Child's Pay: A Cautionary Tale 16
Finding Food for Thought...18
Stone Soup 19
Victims of Love..20
To the Class of 2020 21
The Environmental Science Department 22
Storm Chasing 24
Embattled 25
Beached..26
Pace of Change..27
White America Follows the Pinterest Calendar 28
Wireless Emergency Alert 29
Pandemic Dream #3..30
Masked Advantage 32
A Fifth of July..33
Oh, Say Can You See 34
Why Do I Write Frantically During the Plague.......................................35
Crosses Mark the Passing Year 36

Peace and Harmony

When the panicked uncertainty of first impressions fails to fade,
and seconds tick into second guesses every hour on the hour,
grip tightly onto the hand of stillness.
Feel it hush you away from body and self.
Listen as the mockingbird sings darkness into light,
his repeated repertoire a rosary of prayers
able to steer spinning stars back into predictable orbits.
Down is not drowned.
You will rise again like a tune
joined in harmony with other spheres.

March 15, 2020

In the northern hemisphere, water still spins down the drain clockwise,
March oak pollen yellows
hoods of cars and trucks.
Recycling bins continue to collect empty cups of stale caramel and conversation,
Backyard mockingbirds sing at midnight to hold their turf.
Discolored lint joins cat hair, clumps into laundry room corners.
Silicone cushions press into both sides of your nose, dig shallow pits.
The world goes on- mostly
though just beneath the horizon,
a rising unknown glows
blood red and bloated,
certain as the dawning sun.

Out West

It rose in the east,
a dusty haze first spotted online in alarmist posts,
which too soon shape-shifted itself
into hook echoes on our personal radar.
Ringing warnings spawned awareness
That destruction would surely strike.
But like the town folk in an apocalyptic western,
we lacked the prescience to predict precisely where or when
the outlaw horsemen would arrive.
So we circled the wagons, donned bandanas,
armed ourselves with bleach and hand sanitizer,
hunkered down to await
our doom or rescue.

The Plague

They said it came from Rome
originated in Constantinople.
Called it the Hong Kong flu, the French Disease,
the Spanish Lady.
Blamed it on bad air,
on cats, on dogs, on bats, pangolins, or chimpanzees.

Said it arose due to the curious tastes of Chinese oligarchs
or of peasants in Zimbabwe.
Proclaimed Christ, Mohammed, maybe Aesculapius
sent it down from heaven to punish the faithless.
Or that the devil snuck it in to spread chaos and evil.

Kings and barons spread rumors
Jews spread it through wells
as an excuse to exterminate them,
that slaves were immune
as an excuse to work them to death.
The Pope ignored it, made jokes
as long as it kept its distance.
Treated it with charms and turpentine
behind bird-beaked masks while chanting special masses.

Eventually, the curia defeated it with a tincture
of time and patience, nets and quarantine.
Thus, it disappeared,
making way for new empires, the Renaissance, the Roaring 20's.

The plague smiled and waited
to present itself dressed in new clothes
before a new generation.

Feminine Protection

Friday the 13, 2020.
Mask up- or die! the CDC warned.
Get hold of N-95's,
mysterious protective gear,
named like a gun,
familiar to surgeons,
and those who remove asbestos siding.
Sold out commodities,
harder to score than multipack toilet paper
or jumbo bottles of Purell.

Desperate, we innovated. Badly.

Patty, my sister-in-law, sewed shoestrings
onto cheery calico pouches
she stuffed full of cut-up AC filters
and bent pipe cleaners across the tops
to seal off noses.

I folded layered vacuum cleaner bags
into purple bandanas,
jury-rigged elastic hair ties
to wrap around ears.
My creations were less stylish than Patty's designs,
equally uncomfortable.

Wearing those masks brought back memories
of menarche
in an era before period panties
and womanhood celebrations,
when girls sat bloated and cramped,
doubled over in fear,
as our mothers handed us saddle-sized pads
to pin or strap firmly into place.

Unforgettable, inescapable reminders
of the horrors we could face
should slippage occur.

Angst and Apprehension

Last week my calendar exploded into an annotated maelstrom,
Revisions whirl-winded into reschedules, then cancellations.
But the novelty of chaos kept me afloat.

Now, disaster spins ever faster,
splinters, scatters the scaffolding of our lives,
into pileups of pick-up stick problems.

No one person can sort or cart away.
Big decisions must fall to higher powers.
Jesus take the bulldozer wheel!

Please don't leave the driving to those elected
to fight for the right of each man
to dig his way out of every shit hole
alone.

Supermarket Vision of Hell

Grim go the shoppers to the grocery store,
small apartment people locked down in big towns
who broke out in bawdy song
balanced on balconies the night before.

Today they cue Soviet style in bread lines,
clustering, twisting themselves like mutant RNA
around the block to wait patiently (or not)
for whatever is in store.

Apples, peaches, pears, and plums,
limit 1 bag per customer per trip.
No more blueberry muffins,
the bakery department shut down yesterday.

3 raspberry parfaits and a double Dutch chocolate cake
sit like abandoned puppies in a lone open cooler,
await adoption.

Mice

We walked the dog in the window
of the rushed hour between oncoming storms.
According to the radar, we had time
to escape the indoor Saturday tedium for a few
before the deluge resumed.
Under a cloud-cracked sky in the steam of noon,
everyone and their dog gathered to stream through the park,
to catch the last few sprinkles of exercise
before opportunity drowned in the rain.
Runners, face-masked with determined paranoia,
yanked pit bulls and huskies away from each other,
scurried down trails like animals trapped in a woodland maze.
A redefined rat race for these times.

Living in the Moment

Stuck in the funk of present daze,
I reflexively fish the ever-flowing news stream
as it trickles through a facts-cape where graphs rise and slope into
sameness.
1600 deaths or 6000?
Big numbers numb me to the reality of people's suffering.
But when confronted by a wailing mother
who grieves too long on the morning show,
I flip her off with the remote.

Living in the present daze,
I've learned to suit up, set out to shop scavenger hunt specials.
Week 1 I hoard hand sanitizer,
Week 2 tote truckloads of toilet paper,
Week 3 hanker for ham and home baking supplies.
Now in Week 4, I lust after the blond luster of L'Oreal,
maybe mustache trimmers.

I've quickly learned:
-The measured distance of 6 feet
-How many nanoparticles fabrics can filter
-Origami tricks to folding masks from bandanas
-Ways to zoom into meetings without looking like a potato
-The bandwidth limit of my internet provider
-The bandwidth limit of our patience
  when trying to homeschool an inattentive toddler
-The limited reach of the San Antonio Independent School District,
  which lost contact with 25% of its elementary students
  after Spring Break.

I've discovered I live in a failing state,
a confederacy run by dunces
who insist cities and churches compete reality show style
in a life or death race for resources and respirators.

An environment where community food banks are required
to magically procure loaves and fishes
to feed the Easter multitudes
stalled out for miles along the access road.

José Posada, the Central Market Sax Man

With grace, he grasps the mouthpiece in determined lips
to lead the queued-up passel of passersby
onward through their foggy fears.

He blows his horn
lilting audible kisses,
lifting spirits skyward with high notes.

Salient of the sanctity of the moment,
he soothes all with a balm of song,
a copacetic concoction
of oldies but goodies,
sure to cure with the beatbox
heartbeat of bygone eras.
Syncopation
solders separation into rejoinders of joy.
Someday, it will be okay.

View from my Window

Pictures used to fly into in-boxes
as we flew around the world.
>Diana, bicycling the Italian cobblestone countryside,
>April's husband, canoodling with a kangaroo,
>Priscilla, trekking the Amazon
>>or surrounded by a mountain of Mexican butterflies.

We defined ourselves by distance traveled
Not that this is anything new.
From the 19th century Grand Tour
to 12 countries in 10 days in the 20th
whether guided by Marco Polo or Rick Steves,
oh, the places we'd go.

We're on a different type of journey now,
an artistic retreat which tasks to gather narrative threads,
embroider on the theme of home sweet home.

So, we shoot photos from home.
frame them within the view from my window,
and glimpses from the world of comfortably couched conceits
while we hunker down with a million Facebook friends.

We feel the heaviness of winter in a single morning.
Soggy March snowflakes in the
parking lot
outside a Calgary apartment complex.
See spring begin to pink out from the edges of trees in
Belgium
before bursting into full bloom farther south in Provence and
Tennessee.
We seep into the endless summer green of Sri Lanka and
Cape Town
then arrive with the cooling oranges and brown of earliest autumn near
Wellington.

Across the global picture book, certain images repeat
ocean views and mountains, porticos and patios, repeat.
Window boxes stuffed to overflowing with impatience and phlox,
sunset scenes of the sort which front funeral programs.
Makes me wonder,
are we witnessing the beginning of something or the end?

The Not So Maddening Crowd

I was the cat who walked alone,
the bad mother who never took the kids to Disney
because I refused to brave the lines.
The friend who slithered backward
whenever an old acquaintance spread her arms
and squealed group hug.

Now I dream of being surrounded by crowds,
the warm jostles and overheard conversation
from the 3-generation family celebrating
Easter brunch at the next table.
The shared gasps and laughter
directed at the actors onstage
at a small Sunday matinee.
The rattle and hum
Of 10,000 feet stomping in unison
when the classic rockers jump onstage.

I long for the rustle of song sheets
as the congregation belts out off-key carols
before the manger on Christmas Eve.
Children shouting down polished hallways,
their new sneakers squeaking on the first day of school.
The seventh inning stretch.
The rhythmic jolts as we line dance or slam dance,
or accidentally rub shoulders
when we gather around the club's grungy mirror
to reapply make-up.

I hunger for encounters with coconut-scented tourists
clustered under candy-striped umbrellas,
as boom box reggae or metal music wafts with the waves.
Ache for shared spaces and smiles from familiar strangers.
Should we meet again after this shared isolation ends,
please greet me with more than a nodded hello.

Another Kind of Tragedy

We didn't count on the girl
who became a different type of statistic Monday night.
She'd slipped out to blow off steam,
to escape the hothouse home life.
5 weeks of stay-in-place on-line schooling,
5 weeks without company except her brother and mom,
who nagged her to stay away from friends, to always wear a mask.

Joyriding with a couple of older guys met online,
she never anticipated the gun's presence,
its sudden fire and brimstone explosion.

Maybe they were drunk,
maybe stoned.
Maybe they'd just been playing around.
Local news briefly reported
she had been left bleeding
in a nondescript no man's land behind a strip mall,
before being transferred to University Hospital,
where she died an hour later.

Someday a stranger will unaccountably find himself
facing her grave,
and shake his head knowingly upon reading her date of departure.
He'll walk away, never considering the possibility
she fell victim to a different kind of pandemic.

Rant

Don't deny the need to whine how you've got too much/ too little time,
but don't fall for the line
strung out to trip you up, trip you down and out
on a magic Kool-Aide slide,
no aide to the nurse's aide without PPE,
oh, say can you see, with no end in sight, only a slight
downward turn of the curve, so curb your enthusiasm
in response, as through the wilderness you wander lost,
40 days and 40 nights in quarantine like a suspect ship stuck,
a sitting duck, fear felt for more than the reaper, the keeper
of the key to unravelling the mysteries of RNA
to stop the unravelling of our economy,
not so free to poo-poo the need
to prevent the conflagration of the contagion,
raging and ranging off-base, unmasked, unabashed,
gunning for a fight led by the right, left out
of an American Dream
deferred interest in black lives, which seem matter
as little as those of any redneck mother
of all crises, cry out the hypocrisy decimating our democracy
faster than the virus the world over
what?

Out of Santa Fe

Housekeeping's door rap,
indifferent and efficient,
plunged me into ice water awareness,
aching chills wrapped
within the bleached-out heaviness
of high-end hotel linens.

Vaguely, I recalled checking in sometime after midnight.
2 days after Christmas,
there was no room
at the more reasonably priced inns
as we cross-countried back from Colorado
before the flue could capture another family member.

On spaghetti legs, I docked inside the shower,
sunk onto the cold hardness of its chipped marble floor,
to choke and gagged on stifling steam.
Then swadddled in damp towel clamminess,
fever-spiked hair drenched with sweat,
I teetered on the mattress edge,
connected to the blowdryer's undulating roar
with too a short cord.

For 10 hours, 700 miles, I rode shotgun,
slumped against the truck's window,
propped against the truck's window,
propped up by promises of pillows, warm soup,
and certain recovery.

As we drifted alongside the railroad,
cattle cars and oil tankers snaking past,
I wondered
how long-ago fevered travelers
stayed afloat on their mounts,
survived or died,
pallid pariahs in non-name gulches
sidetracked by typhoid, smallpox, or yellow fever.

Child's Play: A Cautionary Tale

It came on the same way as the time before. Nettie, heavy lidded, sweaty atop the coverlet, propped up against the rounded headboard crowned in walnut curls. Fannie rushed in, the germ of an idea on her lips. "Dolly's sick!"

Nettie moaned as Fannie led her, barefoot and dazed, into the playroom where Dolly lay, still in her box among the birthday wrappings and tissue.

"See the spots? I think it's measles," Fannie declared knowingly. "Go downstairs and grab the tincture of turpentine and a spoon," she ordered. "I'll stay here and sit watch."

Nettie wandered into the kitchen pantry where Mama kept herbs and remedies and then into the dining room to select a baby spoon from inside the velvet lined silver chest. She knew the routine well. A good tonic, a dark room, a few prayers, and her new doll would recover.

But when Nettie returned, Fannie's face turned grim. She'd been wrong. Dolly had the Great Pox. "She mustn't scratch!" the older girl proclaimed. "I need to make her some gloves. Good ones. Not cotton."

Nettie shrugged as she sorted through the dresser in search of one of Mama's church gloves, the ones made from the softest kid. She didn't know why any old gloves wouldn't do. But she was only 5- 6 as of yesterday, June 7, 1898. Fannie, on the other hand, was 10, already an expert at ministering to the sick.

Back in the playroom, Fannie pulled the scissors from her embroidery basket and began to cut up Mama's dress glove. "Machine oil! We must have machine oil for Dolly's hands!" Fannie demanded. "You have to get the oil can from Papa's shed. Hurry!"

Nettie laced up her shoes and headed across the yard, past the chicken coop to the shed where she found the oil can, its thin, greasy neck sticking out above the shelf where the harnesses hung. She grabbed the can and rushed back into the house. But when she arrived back upstairs, Fannie solemnly announced that Dolly was already dead from smallpox.

"No!" Nettie wailed, choking on her words like she had last year when she was down with diphtheria, her throat swelled up and thick as leather. "Why do my dolls always have to die? It's not fair!" "Life may not always seem fair," Fannie reminded her sister. "But who are we to question God's will?"

The girls ceremoniously washed Dolly's face and lay her on a bed of tissue and wrapping paper in the box in which she'd arrived and closed the lid. Tears rolled down Nettie's cheeks as Fannie placed the small package in the ground among the lilies lining the raised blue-floored porch.

Long after her sister had sulked back into the house, Fannie remained outside, swinging her feet off the porch's edge and staring though the waving grass and simmering heat to an ornately iron-fenced square. With sudden determination, she hopped down and began to march along the long drive towards the square, a single lily in her hand.

Sliding, as she always did, through the small side gate- never the big one in front- Fannie walked past rose bushes and dated stones crowned with doves and curls. Finally, she halted in front of a small piece of marble topped with a reclining lamb. There, Fannie leaned forward and whispered, as if to the lamb, "Iris, today I've sent another friend to meet you at Heaven's golden gate."

Finding Food for Thought

Instruction arrives scattershot,
scrambled in bits and bytes drifting through the ether.
Lessons feel lessened,
bring spilt milk tears to the split screen eyes
of students and teachers tiptoeing across eggshells
because misfortune tripped us all.
Shattered conventional assumptions of online learning
we'd foolishly collected in a single basket.

When yolk and white collide, there will be no souffle.
Break a few eggs,
and you can make an omelette.
You may have to scrounge,
from ingredients close at hand.
But with a touch of creativity,
you can whip up into an original dish
to sustain body and spirit
through the hardest of times.

Stone Soup

When life offers only sticks and pebbles,
cobble together a stone soup.
Combine rich flavors into an uncommon collaboration:
Carrots for clear sight and dangled encouragement,
Onions layered in meaning,
Spice of life anecdotes,
Frijoles because we're all full of beans,
Marrow, to remind us
to suck meaning from our bare bones existence,
Peas and hominy to satiate souls.
Create a recipe big enough
to serve all who hunger.

Victims of Love

Confined to close quarters on campus,
at a small school deep in the woods,
they caught feelings.
He was struck first,
no doubt by one of Cupid's unclean arrows.
Soon she felt the same flutter in her chest.

They burned feverishly for a while
aware their condition would prove terminal
(He a senior, she a mere sophomore).
Still, they determined to hold on
—at least until graduation.

In late winter, an unexpected killer appeared,
circling the globe like a vulture
before landing at O'Hare and Heathrow, at LAX, in Rome.
Spreading joy among revelers
along parade routes at Mardi Gras,
lounging beside spring breakers on the Florida sand.

Confined to houses 1000 miles apart,
dizzy from staring at shifting screens
which froze faces in real time,
feelings faltered.
She texted syrupy playlists of love songs,
as last chance sentimental snake oil to rally his failing heart,
but it was too late.

The end came suddenly
during a cold call just before dawn
when she pulled the plug
before he could be the first to whisper forever goodbye

To the Class of 2020
for Andrew as he finished high school

Commencement, what a strange word for graduation. To commence is to begin, what you do after graduation, as in commencing to party hardy with White Claw and Jagermeister as you celebrate your arrival at the point of departure. To leave the nest, fly the coop, soar to success in the adult world.

I've got good news, esteemed members of the Class of 2020: Life has prepared a special gift, just for you! Okay, so it's not what you wanted or expected. But once you unwrap the idea fully, open yourself up to its implications. See you've been given something more valuable than the Apple watch you requested. Best used to tick off quarantined minutes and days. Better than the cherry red jeep with the bow on top you dreamed of-which would have been destined to spend its time stuck in the driveway between Dad's truck and Mom's SUV.

Have a heaping helping of perspective pudding! Sure, it feels like getting a lump of coal in your Christmas stocking. But it's far better to acquire it now before that first job lands you a few spots below the lowest rung on the corporate ladder. Before your best laid plans violently snap shut like a spring-loaded trap leaving you hurt or stranded in some dusty outpost of a far-off land.

Perspective. Not a border internment camp. Not any part of the Middle Ages. Perhaps, you'll come to relish those childish things you deemed ready to be cast away: Family dinners and board games, the comfort of waking up in your old room wrapped in the warm scent of Mom's chocolate chip pancakes. You'll understand why Jane Austen's heroines and pet dogs excitedly anticipate the possibilities offered by daily woodland strolls. Value human interaction, how the girl working drive-through at Chik-Filet says it's been a pleasure to serve you.

The Environmental Science Department at the University of Texas at Austin Holds Graduation Ceremonies 22 May 2020 via Zoom
for Hunter, Maddie, Ryan, Erica, & Dr. Banner

22 faces
in backyards and kitchens,
T-shirts and awkward smiles,
log on, fill the grid.

Department Head without a cap, gown or stole,
top button undone,
waits, stares sidelong at the camera,
oddly focused on his nostrils.

Undergraduate advisor appears postcard-perfect,
saturated in burnt orange paisley,
as UT Tower glows victoriously from behind.

Cue the ceremony's start.

Department Head
commends graduates
for succeeding through 2 months of online classes,
apologizes for the lack of snacks and adult beverages,
served after in-person graduations,
asks students to recall
favorite memories from 4 years of Environmental Science,

Graduates flesh out 4 years of shared stories:
Field work at Port Aransas
capped off by beach bonfires, ghost stories, smores.

A rained-out visit to the Wildflower Center
transformed into a 10-hour night of bowling, fast food burgers,
hide-and-seek.

Environmentally friendly song lyrics
written and performed,
the first assignment for a first semester freshman class
still remembered.

No lectures, readings, or papers written included

in the casual ceremony more meaningful
than Pomp and Circumstance and lockstep sameness
dressed up in caps and gowns.

Storm Chasing

2:00 horizon rises
bubbles white and gray, gold-tipped
with promises of after 5:00 adventures
of rollicking thunder and lightning,
ozone highs.

Gas tank full,
shotgun rider armed with double barrel radar
driver's hands firmly on the wheel, lead foot ready,
we stray north, jig west

Follow skylines of consistently climbing anvils
as cumulous clouds become cumulonimbus
within an atmospheric oven.
Where heat, humidity and pressure gradients
rotate themselves into supercell perfection.

A few miles beyond Mason,
clouds sink,
curtain hills heavily in rainy draperies,
pound the car with Skittles of hail.

Onward we twist
through low clouds, low water crossings,
hooked by radar
on ominous red and green signatures outside Harper.

Gunmetal sky drops buckets of frozen gold balls
across flood puddles, over hood and windshield
as a chorus of banshee phones screams tornado warnings,
commanding us to hightail it back to the highway.

Reflective within the dusty red post-storm sunset,
we recall rollercoaster thrills of the chase behind us,
an adventure enhanced by readouts and radar sites.

Laughing all the way home,
we proclaim storm chasing a good scare, nothing
like the thrumming panic
lived daily within the shadow
of COVID's viral storm.

Embattled

In street corner standoffs
we raise eyebrows
above pale paper shields
inadequate best defense
for the Battle against Covid
in the War on Science.

On the other side,
righteously wrapped in right-wing anger
warriors snarl
rattle sabers from texts
scripted by opportunistic generals
who refuse to take the field.

They charge
barbarians at the gate
aware
invaders and illness
combined forces
drove Rome to its knees.

Beached

The woman behind the register,
unmasked by her smoker's yellow smile,
edges closer like a snake approaching would-be prey.
I slide the gas card onto the counter,
inch away.

You should have seen it in here yesterday, she chortles.
So many customers headed down 37,
off to Corpus, Port A, Padre Island.
Wish I could take time off.
she confidentially sighs,
her sea breeze breath blowing in my direction.
Nodding in feigned agreement,
once again, I step back.

I wish the transaction would go through,
wish to return to the secure isolation of my car,
open the container of disinfecting wipes
waiting silently for me.

Safely behind the wheel,
I watch cars streaming south towards the Gulf.
Shake my head in memory of this morning's posts,
Too many clips glassy-eyed friends
stuffing cars with coolers and umbrellas,
striped towels, 50 SPF sunscreen.

Pace of Change

Change is a bad haircut growing out,
the clean-up after a hurricane,
not the storm itself.

Reformation moves
with caterpillar speed
the time required to transform into a butterfly.

Aspire not
to emerge from emergency
with undo haste.

Wash hands, roll up sleeves,
take to the higher ground

White America follows the Pinterest calendar

> *I can't believe it's already protest season. I haven't taken down my COVID-19 decorations yet. Meme, early June, 2020*

White America follows the news cycle
to decide
which issue to embrace

A June of Nightly Protests
to honor Black Lives destroyed by police brutality?
or a COVID-19
masked and quarantined for 100 days?

White America bleeds years across seasons
into centuries as kings and corporations
pursue plantations and petroleum
which release toxic gases,
raise the planet's temperature,
unleash storms and zoonotic plagues,
pound down hardest upon dehumanized communities.

White America is learning to follow
downward pressure.

Wireless Emergency Alert

Like Cassandra screams
of desperation,
an electric aria
wash over Area Code 210
to disrupt Saturday night
with the shrill energy
last telegraphed
from the Titanic
as the band played on.

Pandemic Dream #3

We stand in a field outside Austin, Texas next to my great-grandparents' house. Roof sagging inward, the dozen white wedding cake columns chipping, fading to gray. Tents and open pavilions scatter among the sparse, summer dry weeds. Area residents, white survivalist types cluster in jury-rigged-every-man-for-himself plots on city fringes. They meander, listen to snake oil salesmen hawk Music Man miracles under little big tops. The locals have organized this convocation to demand a better kind of turf. Grass to carpet bomb their yards suburban dream green. Alive and sweet-smelling. With no need of water or mowing.

I share confused glances with my son, Andrew, and friend, April, who have accompanied me to this improbable gathering. A woman waves us toward a blue and white canopy. It's Annalisa Peace from the Greater Edwards Aquifer Authority. A green island in a dark sea of misinformation/disinformation found! Annalisa beckons us to join a few crunchy, chewy scientific types huddled around a plastic folding table. The experts have a job for us: Go, they say. Scour the earth for sustainable, self-sufficient sod. Find the miracle! Bring it back to us. Save Austin! Save the world!

Andrew, April, and I nod in grim acceptance and march off armed with website addresses, lists of obscure nurseries, and GIS maps which contain botanical information about remote locations. We travel the globe. Traverse shaded valleys. Crawl inside seaside caves. Search the dark web, ancient tombs, and tomes filled with dark magic. Nothing.

Suddenly, Andrew announces he has received a text from the wife of the mayor of Asheville, North Carolina. The mayor knows the secret to humanity's survival. If April will give the man a makeover, his wife will make him spill the beans.

The mayor is a Black man of medium height and build, slightly past middle age, dressed in bureaucratic clothing: creased suit pants, newish loafers, and a starched white dress shirt, sleeves rolled to the elbows. Then there's the hair- a pile of dreadlocks which rises in a coiled tower several inches above his head.

In footage straight off reality TV, April spins the mayor around in a beautician's chair, snaps a waterproof cape around his neck, and goes to work. Snipping scissors and ropes of hair sprawl on the ground. The spiffed-up mayor as he emerges from stage right, dreads now shoulder length in an age-appropriate shade gray, revealing a slightly receded hairline. Wife embraces husband.

The mayor warns that to survive, we must hightail it back to San Antonio and take shelter 600 feet below the Edwards Aquifer. He grabs Andrew by the hand, and they rush south and west. We three women trail after them, running as fast as possible in skirts and heels. Deep below the city, we huddle against sweating rock walls inside a large cavern. Layers of limestone and basalt to a granite batholith studded with giant faceted emeralds. Glowing purple chunks of radioactive fluorite. Suddenly, the space around us groans and rumbles. The world above us explodes with the force of a nuclear bomb.

A muffled whimper emerges from the kitchen. Death and devastation be damned. When a 13-year-old elder pug needs to potty, he needs out now. Springing into action, I rush out of the bedroom, away from my efforts to save the world and open the back door.

Masked Advantage

Isolation is desolation,
contemplation and cogitation
gagged and smothered and masked.

In the confused miasma
of outside contamination,
elastic-bound breathing slows.

Bandanaed within calico constraints,
metamorphoses into an experience
more meditation than suffocation.

Returned to the safety of sequestration,
shields down, inhale sweet and easy,
exhale easy filtered words.

A Fifth of July

Yesterday,
Six Flags and Sea World
hawked last minute splash-time tickets online.
The Botanical Garden
sent me a members' only invitation
to save the date
(and perhaps their bottom line)
for a traditional Independence Day extravaganza.

Last night,
zip-tied Proud Boys
dodged out-of-sight out-of-mind
tear-gassed Indians
to blindly cheer
as the President, backdropped
by Mount Rushmore's
blank-eyed megaliths,
unmasked plans
for a traveling circus
of pop culture with monuments guaranteed
to make America great again.

Today,
I did not drape the dogs in shiny mylar ribbon
for a neighborhood parade.
Saw no need to bake
strawberry spangled flag cake
or stake out my family's claim
in a prime spot to ooh and ahh
fireworks called off
by the cities of San Antonio,
Boerne, Burnet, even
teeny, tiny Bertram.

Tonight,
as the 4th of July fades into the 5th,
neighborhood children
explode through the darkness,
and distract earth and sky with
bottle rockets'

Oh, Say Can You See

America the Badass, the World-Class
Ship of Fools
sails rudderless into the storm,
locks away second-class citizens
to drown like rats.

Tosses empty promised
life jackets overboard,
holds lifeboats in reserve,
like lucky pennies saved
for the chosen few
come this rainy day.

Why Do I Write Frantically During the Plague?

What is this obscene obsession,
this daily drumming on the keys,
the need to battle babbling verbiage
until my streaming thought flow clearly across the screen?

Do I aspire to commit alchemy,
chase the golden goal of turning the experience of a lifetime
into a manuscript perfectly posed for publication?

Am I trying to create a gift for my descendants?
A chronicle of the pandemic
to bind the family narrative
like the Victorian armoire
which survived the 1900 Galveston hurricane.

Or will I choose to squirrel away these papers,
as did my grandfather, who boxed up onion-skinned copies
of 40 years' official correspondence
without apparent cause or order?

Or do I write to give myself a break
from the per diem nothing-better-to-do tedium
of counting days by unstruck hours,
until time's pendulum swings.

Crosses Mark the Passing Year

In March,
we slashed crosses reluctantly
across calendar dates.
Cancellations not countdowns,
ellipses of empty weeks.

In April,
we bore crosses heavy with guilt
after insisting family members
gather to celebrate,
and 8 caught the virus.

A great aunt died, we grieved
her cross among thousands
lined up like poppies
in Flanders Fields.

All summer,
we formed crosses,
arms against chests
to block the evil and misguided
who crossed lines of decency
armed with Molotov hate.

Last November,
we marked crosses
in ballot squares
to choose a better path
at this crisis crossroads of history.

May crosses mark the coming year-
Crosses and crescents
and six-pointed stars
to shine from within,
illuminate our way
with glowing compassion.